REASONS TO CARE ABOUT
WHALES
AND DOLPHINS
[Animals in Peril]

Sara Cohen Christopherson

Enslow Publishers, Inc.
40 Industrial Road
Box 398
Berkeley Heights, NJ 07922
USA
http://www.enslow.com

Library of Congress Cataloguing-in-Publication Data
Christopherson, Sara Cohen.
  Top 50 reasons to care about whales and dolphins : animals in peril / Sara Cohen Christopherson.
     p. cm. — (Top 50 reasons to care about endangered animals)
  Includes bibliographical references and index.
  Summary: "Readers will learn about whales and dolphins—their life cycles, diets, young, habitats, and reasons why they are endangered animals"—Provided by publisher.
  ISBN 978-0-7660-3453-2
  1. Whales—Juvenile literature. 2. Dolphins—Juvenile literature. 3. Endangered species—Juvenile literature. I. Title. II. Title: Top fifty reasons to care about whales and dolphins.
  QL737.C4C53 2010
  599.5—dc22
                              2008048695

Printed in the United States of America

092009 Lake Book Manufacturing, Inc., Melrose Park, IL

10 9 8 7 6 5 4 3 2 1

To Our Readers: We have done our best to make sure all Internet Addresses in this book were active and appropriate when we went to press. However, the author and the publisher have no control over and assume no liability for the material available on those Internet sites or on other Web sites they may link to. Any comments or suggestions can be sent by e-mail to comments@enslow.com or to the address on the back cover.

✪ Enslow Publishers, Inc., is committed to printing our books on recycled paper. The paper in every book contains 10% and 30% post-consumer waste (PCW). The cover board on the outside of each book contains 100% PCW. Our goal is to do our part to help young people and the environment too!

Photographs: Jan Rysavy/iStockphoto, cover inset, 1; Vojtech Soukup/iStockphoto, 1; Doc White/Nature Picture Library, 4, 14, 17, 59, 64, 70; Tom Walmsley/Nature Picture Library, 6; Mark Carwardine/Nature Picture Library, 9, 12, 33, 34, 41, 45, 47, 52, 99; Ruaridh Stewart/AP Images, 10; Pablo Caridad/iStockphoto, 13; Doug Perrine/Nature Picture Library, 18, 84; Jules Kitano/iStockphoto, 21; Xu Jian/Nature Picture Library, 22; iStockphoto, 23, 24 (bottom), 29, 77, 82, 94; Evgeniya Lazareva/iStockphoto, 24 (top); Vicki Beaver/iStockphoto, 27; Solvin Zankl/Nature Picture Library, 28; Debra McGuire/iStockphoto, 30; NOAA National Marine Fisheries Service, 35; Gabriel Rojo/Nature Picture Library, 36, 54; Luke Daniek/iStockphoto, 38; Dale Walsh/iStockphoto, 42; Richard Fitzer/iStockphoto, 44; John Woodcock/Dorling Kindersley, 46; Dorling Kindersley, 49; Robin Dubin/iStockphoto, 50; Patricio Robles Gil/Nature Picture Library, 55; Evgeniya Lazareva/iStockphoto, 56; Mark Soskolne/iStockphoto, 57; Nitin Sanil/iStockphoto, 60; Brett Phibbs/AP Images, 63; Stephan Zabel/iStockphoto, 66; Cheng Chang/iStockphoto, 67; Bullit Marquez/AP Images, 69; Vincent Yu/iStockphoto, 73; Alexander Hafemann/iStockphoto, 74; Peter Scoones/Nature Picture Library, 78, 90; Alan Drummond/iStockphoto, 81; Peter Gordon/Shutterstock Images, 87; Pete Oxford/Nature Picture Library, 88; AP Images, 91; Paul Senyszyn/iStockphoto, 93; Georgette Douwma/Nature Picture Library, 96

Cover caption: A humpback whale breaches near Iceland.
Vojtech Soukup/iStockphoto

CONTENTS

ENDANGERED WHALES AND DOLPHINS

For thousands of years, humans have paid tribute to dolphins and whales in art and legend. We have been awed by the size of whales, particularly the blue whale—the largest animal that has ever lived. We have been intrigued by the playfulness of dolphins.

Centuries of hunting lowered the populations of many large whales, so hunting was banned in the 1980s. Since then, some whale populations have increased, but none have entirely recovered.

Human activities are responsible for most of the current threats to whales and dolphins. Whales and dolphins can be killed if they are caught in fishing gear or exposed to pollution.

Today, many dolphins and whales are endangered. They are listed on the International Union for Conservation of Nature (IUCN) Red List of Threatened Species. All dolphins and whales are protected in U.S. waters under the Marine Mammal Protection Act. Many are also protected by the U.S. Endangered Species Act.

Around the world, people are working to protect whale and dolphin habitats and to prevent accidents with humans. Through the efforts of scientists, governments, organizations, and citizens, dolphins and whales may have a chance.

◀ MANY WHALES AND DOLPHINS ARE ENDANGERED, INCLUDING THIS BLUE WHALE.

GETTING TO KNOW WHALES AND DOLPHINS

REASON TO CARE # I

Whales and Dolphins Are Cetaceans

Whales and dolphins belong to a group of marine mammals called cetaceans. Like humans and other mammals, cetaceans give live birth and nurse their young. They also are warm-blooded, use their lungs to breathe, and have hair. Cetaceans certainly are not furry—but they do have little whiskers, which can be seen especially on young animals.

Dolphins' and whales' bodies are stream-lined for swimming. Instead of arms, they have flippers. Instead of legs, they have powerful tails. All whales live in the ocean, as do most dolphins, though several dolphin species live in rivers.

◀ THIS SEI WHALE, LIKE ALL CETACEANS, IS BUILT TO SWIM.

Whales and Dolphins Are Not Fish

Although they might look like fish, cetaceans are not related to fish at all. One key difference between fish and cetaceans is how they breathe. Fish use gills to take in oxygen directly from the water. Cetaceans swim up to the surface. They breathe in air through their blowholes, which then goes to their lungs.

[Where are a whale's ears? Cetaceans do not have obvious ears that stick out from their bodies. They do, however, have ear parts inside their bodies and can hear very well underwater.]

▶ CETACEANS MUST SURFACE TO BREATHE AIR THROUGH THEIR BLOWHOLES.

REASON TO CARE # 3

Whales and Dolphins Evolved from Land Animals

The ancestors of whales and dolphins were hoofed land animals. These ancient animals lived on land but probably also swam in the ocean, perhaps to hunt. Over millions of years, these land animals evolved into ancient whales that lived their whole lives in the ocean. The oldest whale fossil ever found is more than 53 million years old.

[New studies of genetic evidence suggest that the hippopotamus is the closest relative of whales and dolphins. They may have shared a common ancestor 40 to 60 million years ago.]

◄ SCIENTISTS UNCOVER A WHALE SKELETON BELIEVED TO BE 5 TO 7 MILLION YEARS OLD.

Many Cetaceans Are Endangered

Around eighty species of cetaceans swim in Earth's waters. Of these, at least sixteen are considered endangered or at risk because of shrinking population sizes. One critically endangered dolphin is the baiji. Its scientific name is *Lipotes vexillifer*.

▼ THE BAIJI DOLPHIN IS CRITICALLY ENDANGERED.

▲ A RIGHT WHALE SURFACES OFF THE COAST OF ARGENTINA.

Many whales are also endangered, including blue whales (*Balaenoptera musculus*), fin whales (*Balaenoptera physalus*), sei whales (*Balaenoptera borealis*), and three species of right whales (*Eubalaena glacialis, Eubalaena japonica,* and *Eubalaena australis*).

[Some cetaceans are known by more than one name. The sei whale is also called the coalfish whale.]

REASON TO CARE # 5
Blue Whales
Are Lone Giants

The blue whale is the largest animal that has ever existed—including dinosaurs. It can weigh up to 400,000 pounds (180,000 kilograms) and can be as long as 110 feet (34 meters). An average blue whale is approximately 75 to 100 feet (23 to 30 meters) long and weighs 200,000 to 300,000 pounds (90,000 to 140,000 kilograms)

The blue whale is bluish-gray and patterned with speckles and splotches. Underwater, it often looks a brighter shade of blue. Its small dorsal fin is located near its tail. Blue whales can be found in every ocean except the Arctic Ocean. Blue whales usually live alone or with one other partner. Scientists do not know whether these couples stay together over a long term.

[Blue whales are also the loudest animals on the planet. A blue whale can make a noise that is louder than a jet engine!]

◄ THE BLUE WHALE IS THE LARGEST ANIMAL THAT HAS EVER EXISTED ON LAND OR IN THE SEA.

Fin Whales
Are Multi-colored

The fin whale is the second largest animal that has ever existed. It can weigh as much as 260,000 pounds (120,000 kilograms) and measure up to 90 feet (27 meters) long. A typical fin whale may weigh closer to 100,000 to 140,000 pounds (45,000 to 64,000 kilograms).

The fin whale has a dark gray back and a light underbelly, with a dorsal fin curved back toward the tail. Unlike other whales—as well as most animals—the fin whale has asymmetrical coloration. This means that one side of its body is a different color from the other side. The right side of its jaw is white, but the left side is dark gray or black. The fin whale can be found in every ocean. Generally, it stays far from shore. It does not usually swim in tropical waters.

[Fin whales are social. Although they most often travel alone, they are commonly found in groups of six to ten individuals.]

▶ THE FIN WHALE HAS A DARK BACK AND A LIGHTER-COLORED BELLY.

REASON TO CARE # 7
Sei Whales
Are Speedy

The sei whale can weigh up to 100,000 pounds (45,000 kilograms) and measure up to 66 feet (20 meters) in length. A typical sei whale is about 45 to 55 feet (14 to 17 meters) long and weighs approximately 28,000 to 34,000 pounds (13,000 to 15,000 kilograms). Like the fin whale, the sei whale has a dark gray back and a light underbelly, and its dorsal fin curves back toward its tail.

The sei whale swims faster than other big baleen whales and most cetaceans, too. It reaches speeds of 23 miles per hour. Sei whale travel patterns are mysterious. Many whales may gather in a particular area. Then they might leave and not return for many years. No one knows exactly why. Sei whales can be found in every ocean, but they do not usually venture into polar waters.

[Sei whales usually swim alone or in small groups. They are often called "the greyhound of the sea" because they swim so quickly.]

◀ A SEI WHALE SWIMS WITH HER CALF.

Right Whales Have White Spots

Right whales consist of several different species, but they all look similar. These whales got their name because the slow swimmers were considered the "right" whales to hunt.

A right whale weighs up to 200,000 pounds (90,000 kilograms) and can be as long as 60 feet (18 meters). A typical right whale weighs 40,000 to 60,000 pounds (18,000 to 27,000 kilograms). Its black body has white areas on the belly and thick patches of skin on the head. Called callosities, the patches are found above the eyes and around the mouth.

Right whales will not swim in tropical waters. Species in the southern hemisphere and in the northern hemisphere are kept separate by the warm water between them. The three species of right whales are the North Atlantic right whale, the North Pacific right whale, and the Southern right whale.

[Some fish, whales, and dolphins have dorsal fins on their backs. Right whales have no dorsal fins at all.]

► RIGHT WHALES HAVE WHITE SPOTS ON THEIR HEADS AND NO DORSAL FINS.

Dolphins Live in Oceans and Rivers

Dolphins are much smaller than most whales. Most dolphins are light gray on top and white underneath. A dolphin has a long, narrow mouth, called a beak, and a round forehead, or melon. It has wide flippers and a low dorsal fin near the middle of its back. Most dolphins live in the ocean, but some live in freshwater rivers.

▼ THE BAIJI DOLPHIN IS CALLED THE "GODDESS OF THE YANGTZE."

▲ THE YANGTZE IS THE LONGEST RIVER IN CHINA AND ALSO THE THIRD LONGEST RIVER IN THE WORLD.

The baiji dolphin is found only in the Yangtze River in China and has been nicknamed the "Goddess of the Yangtze." Baiji dolphins are about 8 feet (2.4 meters) long and weigh 280 to 370 pounds (130 to 170 kilograms).

[Social dolphins live in groups with dozens of individuals. Dolphin and whale groups are known as pods.]

WHALE AND DOLPHIN BIOLOGY

REASON TO CARE # 10

Cetaceans Come in Different Sizes

The smallest of the baleen whales, the pygmy right whale, is still quite large. It can reach 21 feet (6 meters) in length, which is still about half as long as a school bus. The largest known whale, the blue whale, is usually about as long as two school buses.

The smallest dolphin is only 4 to 5 feet (1.2 to 1.5 meters) long and weighs about 120 pounds (50 kilograms). That is smaller than many adult humans. The orca, or killer whale, is actually a dolphin, not a whale. At 30 feet (9 meters) long and more than 12,000 pounds (5,400 kilograms), it is the largest dolphin. The most familiar dolphin, the bottlenose, is approximately 10 feet (3 meters) long and weighs 1,000 pounds (450 kilograms). Porpoises are a third type of cetacean. They are smaller than most dolphins.

◀ TOP: THE ORCA IS A LARGE DOLPHIN. BOTTOM: THE BOTTLENOSE IS THE BEST-KNOWN DOLPHIN.

Some Cetaceans Have No Teeth

Cetaceans can be divided into two main groups, those with teeth and those with baleen. All dolphins and some whales have teeth. The blue, fin, sei, and right whales are baleen whales. Toothed cetaceans catch fish and other prey a few at a time. Baleen whales, on the other hand, use their baleen to filter huge quantities of small plants and sea creatures from the water.

Baleen is made of long rows of stiff but flexible material, similar to fingernails. Baleen works like a giant filter to separate small prey from the ocean water. Baleen whales have folds, called ventral ridges, along their throats. These unfold to expand the whale's throat when it gulps a mouthful of food.

[The exact size and shape of baleen is different in each species, depending on what the whale eats.]

▶ THIS FIN WHALE'S BALEEN COMES DOWN FROM ITS TOP JAW; ITS THROAT BULGES BELOW AS IT FILLS WITH WATER.

Baleen Whales
Eat Krill

Baleen whales eat krill and other tiny ocean organisms. Krill are similar to tiny shrimp. They are only 1 or 2 inches long. They gather in huge swarms. This makes it easy for whales and other sea animals to eat big mouthfuls at a time. Some whales, including fin and sei whales, may feed on small fish, such as herring and anchovies, which travel in large groups, called schools.

▼ TINY KRILL ARE EATEN BY MANY LARGER OCEAN ANIMALS, INCLUDING WHALES.

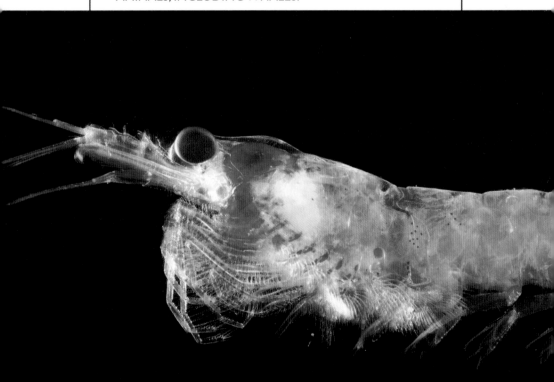

▲ HUNDREDS OF ANCHOVIES IN A SCHOOL MOVE ALMOST AS ONE.

[Blue whales can fit 2,200 pounds of krill in their stomachs—about the weight of a small car!]

REASON TO CARE # 13

Dolphins Are Good at Finding Food

Like other toothed cetaceans, dolphins hunt fish or squid. Sometimes dolphins hunt in groups. They attack from all sides to round up a school of fish. Clumped in a tight ball, the fish become easy prey.

Some dolphins have been seen using sponges—soft ocean animals—to protect their beaks while they poke around for food in rocky areas. Researchers think that mother dolphins teach this trick to their offspring, as baby dolphins have been spotted with sponges covering their beaks.

[Dolphins have cone-shaped teeth. Their teeth are for catching and killing prey, not for chewing. Dolphins swallow their food whole or in big chunks.]

◀ RESEARCHERS BELIEVE DOLPHINS TEACH THEIR CALVES HOW TO FIND FOOD.

Whales Make Huge Spouts

Instead of nostrils, cetaceans have one or two blowholes located at the very top of their heads. This allows the animal to just barely break the surface of the water to breathe. As the blowhole comes up, the animal inhales and exhales. As a cetacean exhales, it releases a spray of moist air, called a spout or blow.

Whale species can be identified by the shape and size of their spouts. Blue whales have enormous spouts, shooting straight up for 30 feet. Fin whales' spouts are somewhat shorter, reaching 20 feet. Sei whales blow only 10 feet high. A right whale makes a low, wide V-shaped spout from its two widely spaced blowholes.

[Baleen whales have two blowholes. Toothed cetaceans have only one blowhole.]

▶ A BLUE WHALE'S SPOUT CAN SPRAY AS HIGH AS 30 FEET.

Blubber Has Several Uses

Cetaceans have a layer of fat just beneath their skin. This layer, called blubber, helps to keep the animal warm. The fat also stores energy. In the past, humans used blubber for food, particularly in small coastal villages and communities around the world. It was burned to fuel lamps for light and also used in beauty products. Blubber was one of the reasons whale hunting was so profitable.

▼ WHALES HAVE A THICK LAYER OF WHITE BLUBBER UNDER THEIR SKIN.

▲ IN THIS ENGRAVING, WHALERS HAVE HARPOONED A WHALE IN ORDER TO KILL IT.

In past centuries, blubber was so valuable it was called "liquid gold."

REASON TO CARE # 16
Whales
Have Lice

Whales have parasites that live on their bodies, eating the whales' dead skin cells. Because these parasites resemble the lice that can live on humans, they are known as whale lice. But whale lice are not really lice—they are tiny crab-like animals called cyamids. Whale lice attach to thick patches of skin on a whale's head. They make white clusters that stand out against the whale's darker skin. Whales can be identified by the particular patterns of their cyamids.

Whale lice stay on their whale for their entire lives. One whale can be home to more than seven thousand cyamids!

◀ THE HEAD OF THIS SOUTHERN RIGHT WHALE IS HOME TO MANY CYAMIDS.

REASON TO CARE # 17

Dolphins Are Fast Learners

In general, dolphins have big brains for their body size, and dolphins are known to be quite intelligent. In captivity, dolphins have been trained to communicate with humans through whistles and body language.

Karen Pryor, cofounder of Hawaii's Sea Life Park and Oceanic Institute, showed that it took about the same amount of time to train humans and dolphins to do a new trick. She wanted to prove the dolphins' intelligence. Pryor presented both groups with a series of tricks. It took awhile for both the humans and the dolphins to catch on, and both became frustrated. Both groups learned the tricks in about the same amount of time. Both groups were excited about their accomplishments. Pryor showed that dolphins and humans behave in some similar ways when they are learning new things.

◀ THIS CAPTIVE DOLPHIN PERFORMS A TRICK.

Whales and Dolphins Have Feelings

Scientists believe that cetaceans experience emotions, just as humans do. When two dolphins are separated, they sometimes show sadness. When reunited, they will often act excited or happy.

Cetaceans might be able to feel emotions because of their brains, which share similarities with human brains. Spindle cells are a type of brain cell once thought to exist only in the brains of humans and apes. Recently, scientists discovered that whales and dolphins also have spindle cells. These cells are important for learning, communicating, and cooperating—and may be related to emotion as well. Spindle cells might also help animals think quickly by connecting different areas of their large brains.

[Unlike most animals, dolphins can recognize themselves in the mirror. This self-awareness is considered a sign of intelligence.]

▶ TWO FIN WHALES SWIM TOGETHER. SOME CETACEANS SHOW SADNESS WHEN SEPARATED FROM EACH OTHER.

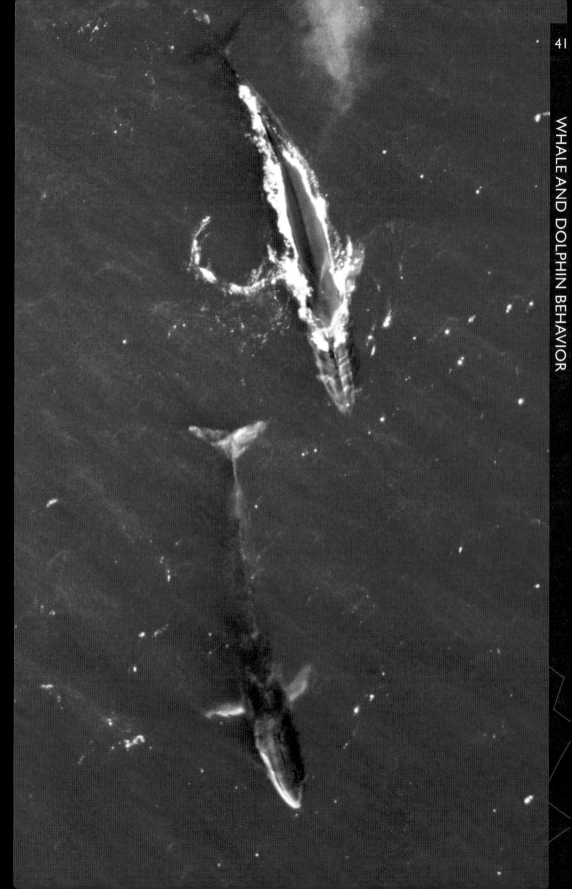

Whales and Dolphins Make a Big Splash

Breaching is when a cetacean jumps all the way out of the water and flops back in the water on its belly or back. It comes down with a splash and a loud slap. Smaller dolphins can easily leap entirely out of the water. Most larger whales can jump out, too. The blue whale, however, is so large that it can only jump out partway.

Whales might breach just for fun, or breaching might have a practical purpose. Hitting the water hard might help to remove parasites on a cetacean's skin. The splash and noise might also warn other animals to stay out of the whale's territory.

◄ A HUMPBACK WHALE BREACHES NEAR HAWAII.

Whales and Dolphins Have Smooth Moves

Fluking, lobtailing, spyhopping, and flipper-flopping: These fun words are actual terms. They describe ways that whales and dolphins move. Fluking is when an animal lifts its fluke, or tail, out of the water. Slapping the fluke against the water is called lobtailing. Spyhopping is when a cetacean pops its head out of the water while keeping its body straight up and down. When a whale slaps one of its flippers against the water surface, it is flipper-flopping.

▼ THIS BLUE WHALE IS FLUKING: LIFTING ITS TAIL OUT OF THE WATER.

▲ THIS SPERM WHALE IS LOGGING, OR FLOATING AT THE SURFACE OF THE WATER.

REASON TO CARE # 21

Whales and Dolphins Sleep Underwater

Humans and other land animals don't have to think about breathing, even while they sleep. But whales and dolphins must control their blowholes. They must be careful to open their blowholes only at the surface. How do cetaceans sleep and still remember to breathe? Some cetaceans may rest only half of the brain at a time. The other half stays awake to control breathing—and to stay alert for danger. Cetaceans may also sleep while logging, or floating at the water surface. Scientists do not yet fully understand exactly how this works.

REASON TO CARE # 22

Dolphins Navigate with Echoes

All cetaceans use echolocation to some extent, but dolphins do so extensively. They can use echoes to find even small and faraway items, such as prey. How does this work? A dolphin makes clicking noises that travel as sound waves through the ocean. If the waves hit an object, they echo, or bounce back. If the object is nearby, the echo happens quickly. If the object is far away, the echo takes longer. Either way, the process occurs very quickly.

▼ CETACEANS USE ECHOLOCATION TO FIND ANIMALS AND OBJECTS IN THE WATER.

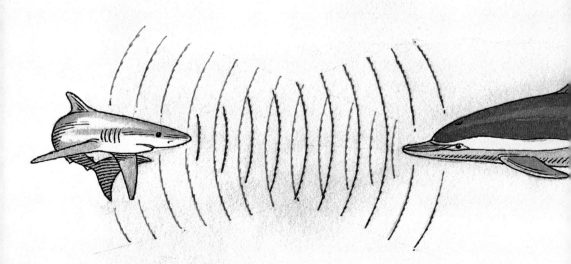

▲ THE BAIJI DOLPHIN RELIES ON ECHOLOCATION.

[The baiji dolphin's tiny eyes cannot see much in the muddy
waters of the Yangtze River. It makes up for this lack of vision
by using echolocation to find its way.]

Whales Have Deep Voices

Cetaceans make some sounds for echo-location. Other sounds are for communication. Underwater, sound waves can travel very far. Fin, blue, right, and other whales are all quite vocal. Their low noises, or vocalizations, can be heard hundreds—and even thousands—of miles away.

Scientists use acoustic tags to record whale sounds. Tags are attached to a whale's back with a suction cup. After the tag falls off, it can be located through radio signals. Humans are still trying to understand why whales make sounds and what the sounds mean. Whale vocalizations probably share information about food sources, mating, and other social activities.

[The humpback whale is a baleen whale famous for its beautiful and haunting "singing."]

▶ WHALES CAN COMMUNICATE ACROSS LONG DISTANCES.

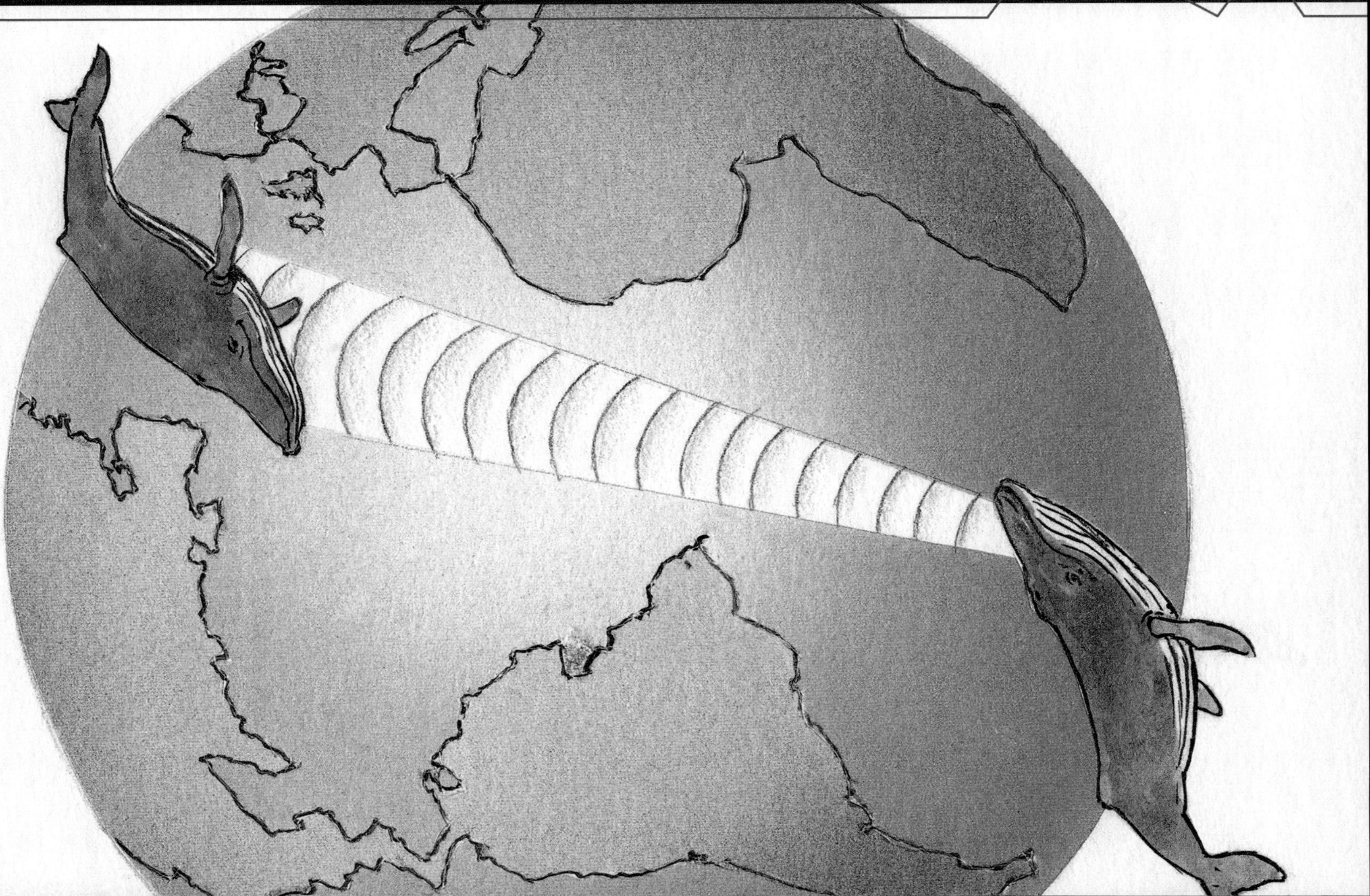

REASON TO CARE # 24

A Mystery Whale
Roams the Pacific

Each whale species makes its own sounds. Whale calls may tell when food or danger is near, but no human knows what the calls mean. Using underwater recording, researchers can recognize whales by the unique pitch of their calls. The call of a fin whale, for example, is around 20 hertz. Blue whales call at 15 to 20 hertz.

For more than seventeen years, one whale in the Pacific has been calling at 52 hertz. Each year, this same whale has been recorded—but never seen. No species of whale is known to sing quite like this one. It also migrates on a different schedule from any other known species.

Scientists do not know what to make of this mystery whale. It might be one individual from a known species that just behaves differently. Or, it could be an unknown species, yet to be discovered.

[Hertz is the unit that is used to measure pitch, or how high or low a sound is. Hertz measures the frequency of sound vibrations per second.]

◀ WHALES GATHER TO FEED TOGETHER.

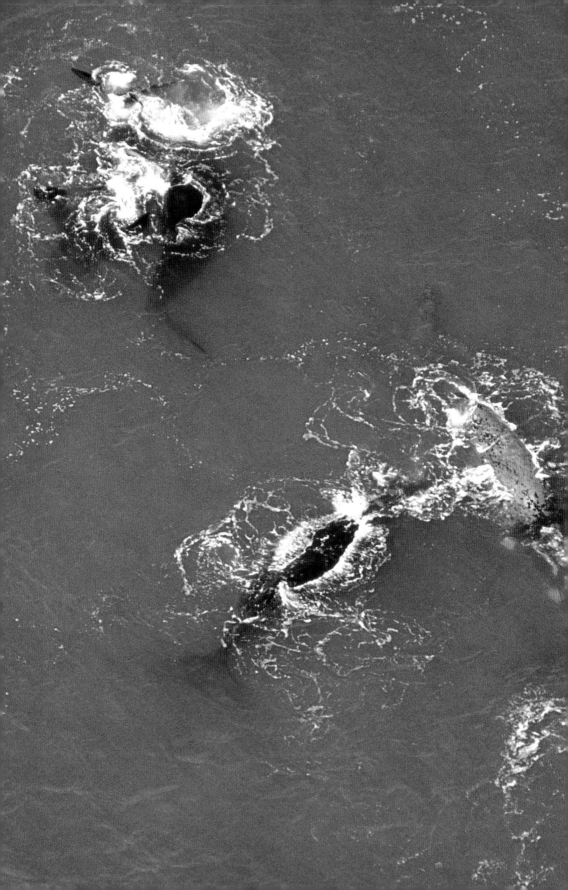

WHALE AND DOLPHIN LIFE CYCLES

REASON TO CARE # 25

Whales Travel for Breeding and Feeding

Some species of whales migrate with the seasons. They migrate to find food, as well as to breed and birth, or calve. For many species, this migration occurs during the winter.

A baby whale develops inside its mother for around twelve months before birth. This is why breeding and calving occur at the same time of year. Breeding one year means a baby whale the next year.

Not all whales migrate seasonally. Also, the exact movements of some whales, including fin and sei whales, are not entirely understood. Sei whales are thought to migrate seasonally, but their movement is not always predictable. Fin whales do not migrate in any regular pattern.

◀ A GROUP OF SOUTHERN RIGHT WHALES COMES TOGETHER FOR MATING.

REASON TO CARE # 26

Whales and Dolphins
Have Belly Buttons

Like other mammals, whales and dolphins give birth to their young. Inside its mother's womb, a baby cetacean is nourished through its umbilical cord. After the cetacean is born, its cord falls off. The baby's belly button marks where the umbilical cord was attached. After birth, a baby cetacean must surface quickly to draw its first breath of air. The mother will help, guiding her baby up to the water's surface.

▼ WHALE MOTHERS GUIDE THEIR NEWBORN CALVES TO THE SURFACE TO BREATHE.

▲ WHALE CALVES STAY CLOSE TO THEIR MOTHERS.

REASON TO CARE # 27

Baby Whales
Are Big

At birth, a typical human baby weighs about 7 pounds (3 kilograms). In contrast, a newborn blue whale can weigh 4,000 pounds (1,800 kilograms)! Feeding only on its mother's milk, a baby blue whale gains around 200 pounds each day. Similar to humans, cetaceans usually have one baby at a time. A baby whale is called a calf. Calving is another word for whale birthing.

Depending on the species, a baby cetacean may nurse for months or years before it begins to eat solid food. A mother cetacean might not sleep at all during the first month after giving birth. She stays alert, protecting her baby at all hours.

Young Cetaceans Face Predators

A full-grown whale has few predators (besides humans), but young cetaceans are vulnerable to attack. Because sharks and orcas both prey on young whales, the calves stay close to their mothers for protection. But all whales—even blue whales—can be attacked by orcas. Some whales have scars from attacks they have survived.

▼ ORCAS PREY ON YOUNG WHALES.

▲ THE GREAT WHITE SHARK IS ONE OF THE MOST FEARSOME PREDATORS IN THE OCEAN.

[A baby whale also stays close to its mother because it is easier to swim in her wake.]

Whales Live Long Lives

Scientists can estimate the age of individual whales, but the exact lifespan of most whales is unknown. Fin and blue whales can live more than ninety years, while sei and right whales can live to be more than seventy. Bowhead whales might be the longest living mammals. Living bowheads have been found with one-hundred-year-old harpoons inside their bodies.

The age of a whale can be estimated by studying certain molecules in the whale's eyes. These molecules change at a known rate. The older the whale, the more the molecules have changed. This method found one bowhead whale that lived to be more than two hundred years old.

▶ MOLECULES IN A WHALE'S EYES CAN TELL SCIENTISTS THE AGE OF THE WHALE.

WHALES AND DOLPHINS IN CULTURE

REASON TO CARE # 30

Dolphins Have Been Used as Symbols

Dolphins have been admired since ancient times. Sailors believed that dolphins were good luck. Spotting a dolphin meant good weather was ahead. Dolphins in Greek mythology were connected with the sea god, Poseidon. In India, the Ganges River dolphin was associated with the Hindu river goddess. Many ancient cultures also depicted dolphins on coins.

Today, dolphins still appear as symbols of life, energy, and intelligence. One very familiar dolphin is the mascot of the Miami Dolphins football team.

[A constellation is a pattern of stars in the sky. The constellation delphinus, the dolphin, was named in ancient times. According to one myth, the constellation was named in honor of a dolphin sent by the Greek god Apollo to save a drowning sailor.]

◀ THIS MODERN STATUE OF POSEIDON STANDS IN VIRGINIA BEACH, VIRGINIA.

Whales Inspired Maori Legend and Lore

The Maori people have lived in New Zealand for around one thousand years. In Maori legend, whales served as guides, or *kaitiaki*, for sailors in canoes. Maori legends also tell of people riding whales. The story of Paikea tells about the origins of a group of native New Zealanders, the Ngati Konohi. According to legend, their original ancestor, Paikea, arrived in New Zealand on the back of a whale.

The 2002 movie *Whale Rider* takes place in a contemporary Maori village. Tradition says that the village's people are descended from Paikea.

▶ THESE MAORI WARRIORS ARE DRESSED TO PARTICIPATE IN A TRADITIONAL CEREMONY.

REASON TO CARE # 32

Whales Are Important in Inupiat Tradition

The Inupiat Eskimos are native Alaskan people. For thousands of years, they have hunted whales for food. Today, whaling is still an important part of their survival and culture. Before the whaling season begins, the Inupiat perform many traditional customs. One custom is to make an offering to the moon and ask it for good hunting.

When the whales begin to pass by shore on their seasonal migration, everyone hopes to spot the first one. When the first whale is seen, a cheer begins, "*Puiyaqpulguuq! Puiyaqpulguuq!*" This means, "The whales are blowing!"

[The native tribes of northern Alaska, Canada, and Greenland are known as either Eskimo or Inuit, depending on the specific tribe.]

◄ A MEMBER OF A NATIVE ARCTIC TRIBE STANDS NEAR HIS KAYAK WITH A TRADITIONAL HARPOON.

Dolphins and Whales
Live in Captivity

Some dolphins can survive and reproduce in captivity. For other cetaceans, captivity is simply impractical. It's nearly impossible to build a tank large enough for a blue whale.

[Captive cetaceans live in aquariums. Aquariums that specialize in dolphins are called dolphinariums.]

▼ DOLPHINS SWIM ALONG THE WALL OF THEIR TANK.

▲ ORCAS IN CAPTIVITY CAN BE TRAINED TO DO TRICKS.

Captive cetaceans provide entertainment for visitors, doing tricks and performing in shows. Aquariums also provide educational opportunities for visitors to learn more about marine animals. Most aquariums are involved in conservation efforts and work to protect cetaceans in the wild. Aquariums may also help to treat sick or injured cetaceans. However, some cetaceans have trouble reproducing in captivity.

Dolphins Are Rescuers

From time to time, stories about dolphins saving humans appear in the news. Sometimes, dolphins protect swimmers or surfers from shark attacks. They rescue people who are shipwrecked or drowning. Dolphins have been helping humans for centuries. Ancient Greek stories also tell of dolphins saving people from drowning. Dolphins on ancient coins are often depicted with humans riding their backs.

In March 2008, it seemed likely that two whales stuck on a New Zealand beach were going to die. As people were giving up hope, a dolphin swam up to the whales and appeared to communicate with them. Within minutes, the whales were swimming off into the ocean. Of course, no one knows what happened for certain. But it certainly looked as if the dolphin saved the whales.

[Dolphins might appear friendly, but they are wild animals. Do not approach dolphins without expert supervision.]

▶ CAPTIVE DOLPHINS DEMONSTRATE HOW TO SAVE A PERSON FROM DROWNING.

THREATS TO WHALES AND DOLPHINS

REASON TO CARE # 35

Cetaceans Face Possible Extinction

The International Union for the Conservation of Nature (IUCN) publishes the IUCN Red List, which defines the conservation status of species as vulnerable, endangered, or critically endangered. It also explains how each animal or plant is being protected. A vulnerable species is at high risk of extinction. An endangered species is at very high risk of extinction. A critically endangered species is at extremely high risk of extinction. Cetacean populations are still recovering from centuries of whale hunting. Today, they are still threatened by human activities. They can be accidentally killed by fishing gear, ships, and pollution.

Blue, fin, sei, North Atlantic right, and North Pacific right whales are all endangered. The Southern right whale's IUCN status ranks at the least concern level. But the baiji dolphin is critically endangered.

◄ THE SOUTHERN RIGHT WHALE IS IN LESS DANGER OF EXTINCTION THAN SOME CETACEANS.

The Baiji Might Already Be Extinct

Sadly, the baiji dolphin might already be extinct. The Yangtze River is heavily used by humans. Baiji dolphins are threatened by boat traffic, pollution, and loss of food. Buildings and dams are also destroying their habitat.

In 2006, a group of researchers traveled the Yangtze River. They looked for the dolphin, and they listened for the dolphins' sounds using underwater sensors. After six weeks, they had not seen or heard any baiji dolphins.

In 2007, a local resident took a video of a large, pale animal that researchers confirmed was a baiji dolphin. Clearly, only a very small number of individuals remain. Such a small population means the species has very little chance for survival. If it becomes extinct, the baiji will be the first cetacean driven to extinction by human activity.

▶ THIS BAIJI DOLPHIN MIGHT BE ONE OF THE LAST OF ITS SPECIES. IT WAS PHOTOGRAPHED IN 2000.

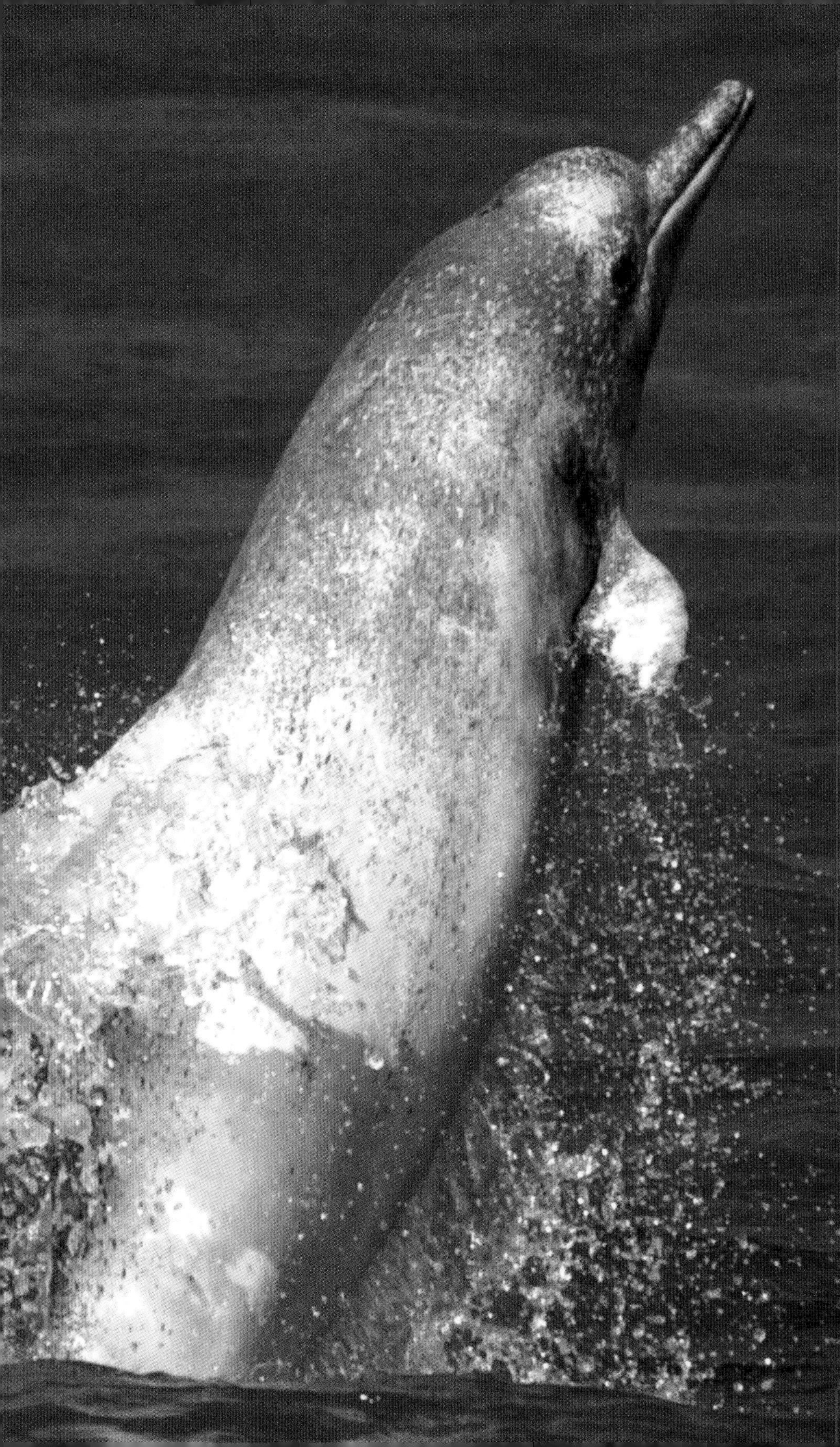

REASON TO CARE # 37
Commercial Whaling
Took Its Toll

Before the second half of the twentieth century, unlimited whale hunting greatly reduced the populations of many species. In 1966, humpback whaling was banned worldwide. In 1986, the killing of other whales in most circumstances was outlawed.

Scientists do not know whether some whales, such as the sei whale, have increased in numbers since then. Other whales, such as the blue whale, are recovering in some waters but not in others. Almost all whale populations have suffered a loss from human activity. Only one species of whale, the minke whale, is thought to have a stable population.

[Although protected from most hunting, whales and dolphins are still killed by accident. Cetaceans get tangled in fishing nets or hit by boats. Some scientists estimate that one-third of all right whale deaths are caused by humans.]

◀ AN ABANDONED WHALING BOAT RUSTS IN SOUTH GEORGIA, NEAR ANTARCTICA.

Ocean Changes Affect Cetaceans

Ocean pollution affects all marine life, including cetaceans. Large quantities of harmful pesticides, chemicals, and other toxins have washed in or been dumped into the oceans. These pollutants are taking their toll.

Because they live so long, cetaceans are exposed to pollutants over many decades. Scientists worry that certain pollutants could interfere with the animals' life cycles. The chemicals cause birth defects and might cause disease. These pollutants could also make it difficult for cetaceans to mate successfully.

Climate change may also harm whales and dolphins. Changing water temperatures affect the cetaceans' ecosystems. This harms the animals by altering food supplies, among other things.

[Some cetaceans have died after mistaking plastic bags for food and swallowing them.]

▶ CHANGING WATER TEMPERATURES COULD MAKE IT MORE DIFFICULT FOR CETACEANS TO SURVIVE.

REASON TO CARE # 39

Whale Food Is in Danger

Krill are part of the base of the ocean food web. Many animals, including birds, fish, seals, and whales, rely on krill for food. People also use krill as food, as a health supplement, and as feed for fish and livestock. Thousands of tons of krill are harvested from the ocean each year, and the harvests are increasing. Scientists worry that humans will leave too little krill to support the ocean food web.

Krill numbers also might be dropping because of climate change. Krill depend on the algae that grow under polar sea ice. As the sea ice shrinks, there is less food for krill.

Protecting whales requires protecting whales' habitats—including their food sources. The Antarctic Krill Conservation Project is one organization working to protect krill.

◀ THE OCEAN FOOD WEB DEPENDS ON KRILL.

Beached Whales
Often Die

No one knows exactly what causes whales to beach. Most types of cetaceans are known to beach, but it is a more common problem for toothed whales and dolphins. If a whale beaches, it might get too dry and die.

Cetaceans have beached after exposure to sonar from naval ships. But not all incidents of beaching are caused this way. Historical records document stranded whales from hundreds of years ago, which suggests the problem is not caused only by modern human activity. Whales also beach if they are ill or lost.

[River dolphins and dolphins that live in shallow waters near the shore do not seem to have problems with beaching.]

▶ SOMETIMES WHALES BEACH FOR NO OBVIOUS REASON.

Human Noise May Block Cetacean Communication

Humans have made the ocean a very noisy place. Huge ships rumble, engines roar, and naval boats send sonar blasts. For cetaceans, communication may be like trying to talk in a crowded gymnasium. The noise also interferes with the animals' abilities to echolocate, or listen to echoes to find their way through the water.

Ships and submarines use sound waves called sonar to detect other ships and locate the ocean floor. Sonar might be dangerous for cetaceans. It could damage cetaceans' ears to the extent that the animals can no longer use echolocation to find their way around. It may even cause internal bleeding. Injured, and without the ability to navigate, the animals could get stranded on shore and die. In many different areas, cetaceans have been found stranded with ear damage after swimming through sonar. Recent laws limit the use of sonar to protect cetaceans.

[Male fin and blue whales are thought to attract mates with a sort of "song." Their songs can travel thousands of miles—if not blocked out by other noises.]

◄ THE SONAR FROM HUMAN SHIPS MIGHT MAKE IT DIFFICULT FOR WHALES TO COMMUNICATE.

WHALE AND DOLPHIN CONSERVATION

REASON TO CARE # 42

Whales and Dolphins Face a Changing Environment

Last century, cetacean populations were devastated by hunting. Blue, fin, sei, and right whale populations today are just a small fraction of the sizes they were before commercial whaling. Although the practice is banned now, the future still holds many challenges. Cetaceans can be hit by boats or tangled in fishing gear. They must survive ocean pollution and climate change. If current trends continue, some scientists predict that certain species of whales will become extinct within the next two centuries.

With ongoing global efforts to protect cetaceans, there is still hope that their populations will rebound. Their survival depends on the health of the oceans' ecosystems. Setting up marine sanctuaries, where ocean life is protected, is one way to safeguard cetaceans.

◀ THE SURVIVAL OF WHALES SUCH AS THIS SEI WHALE DEPENDS ON HEALTHY OCEANS.

Whaling Laws
Limit Whale Hunting

The International Whaling Commission formed in 1946. In 1986, commercial whaling was banned. Even today, not everyone agrees with the ban. Although some whaling continues—both legally and illegally—whale hunting is currently less of a threat to whales than accidental death from other human-related hazards.

The Japanese government carries out scientific whaling, killing whales in order to study them. The meat is then sold in Japan. Scientists are deeply divided on this issue. Some argue that limited killing of whales is necessary to study them. Others think that whales should be studied without being killed. Some environmental groups charge that scientific whaling is an excuse to hunt whales and serves no scientific purpose.

[Some traditional communities, including the Inupiat Eskimos, may still hunt whales legally. Even so, they may only hunt a certain number of whales each year.]

▶ WHALE MEAT FOR SALE AT A JAPANESE MARKET

Whaling Is Important to Coastal Cultures

Some coastal communities have hunted whales for thousands of years, and whaling is still central to their cultures and traditions. Whale meat is also an important source of food in some places.

Alaskan Eskimos are allowed to hunt the bowhead whale. The Alaska Eskimo Whaling Commission protects traditional whaling practices of the Inupiat and Siberian Yupik Eskimos who live along the northern Alaskan coast. The commission also works to protect whale habitats.

The Eskimos eat many parts of the whale, including the meat, organs, and *muktuk*—the layer of blubber and skin. Other parts of whales are used for other purposes. When a whale is killed, its meat and products are shared with the entire community.

◄ A YUPIK ESKIMO MAN FISHES USING TRADITIONAL METHODS.

Fishing Rules
Protect Whales

The Atlantic Large Whale Take Reduction Plan was started by the U.S. government in 1997. It outlines rules intended to protect whales from commercial fishing. The plan includes making changes to commercial fishing equipment so that cetaceans can escape if accidentally caught. If a whale is tangled in fishing gear, the accident is reported and experts come to free the whale. Also, certain types of fishing are not allowed in locations where whales gather.

▼ THIS GRAY WHALE DIED AFTER IT BECAME TANGLED IN A FISHING NET.

▲ SCIENTISTS TAG A BELUGA WHALE.

REASON TO CARE # 46

Whales and Dolphins Are Tracked by Satellite

Scientists want to learn more about cetaceans. But whales are very difficult to observe directly. Scientists attach satellite tags to whales and dolphins to learn more about them. The tag is a small device that tracks an animal's movements using satellite signals.

In 2004, a tagged right whale led researchers to a group of other right whales. At least seventeen right whales had gathered there. It was a hopeful sign for this endangered species.

Scientists Study Whale Feces

By studying whale feces, or poop, scientists can discover all sorts of information. Feces can contain genetic information, bacteria, and toxins. Scientists can learn whether a whale is pregnant, what it has been eating, and many other details.

Rosalind Rolland, a scientist at the New England Aquarium, studies right whale feces. She collects samples by boat. Dogs trained to smell whale feces from the boat lead her to the samples. Her research has provided critical information about these endangered whales.

[Some whales release feces when they feel threatened. The dark, cloudy water hides the whale while it escapes.]

▶ SCIENTISTS CAN ALSO LEARN A LOT FROM BEACHED DEAD WHALES.

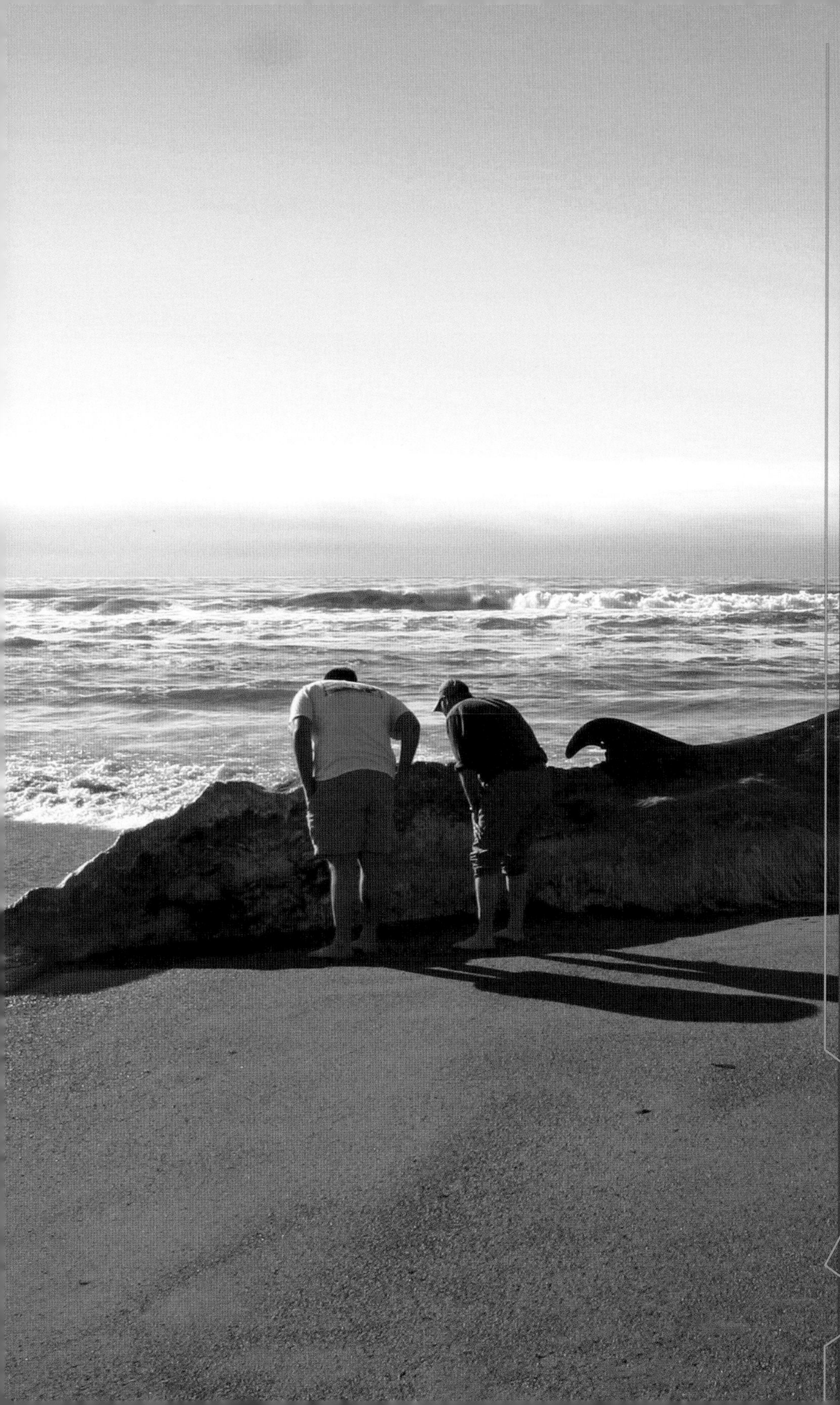

Tourism
Raises Awareness

Today, whale- and dolphin-watching tours are big business. Tourists travel around the world for a chance to see cetaceans in natural habitats. Many coastal communities have found that tourism brings in more money than whaling ever did. Tours also can be good for whales and dolphins. Learning about cetaceans and seeing them in the wild inspires many people to work harder to protect them. The communities that rely on tourism will work harder to protect whales and dolphins, too.

However, tours must be managed carefully. Scientists worry that tours can disrupt cetaceans' normal ways of life. The International Whaling Commission and many countries have published guidelines for whale and dolphin viewing. They warn that cetaceans must be allowed to approach boats on their own and should never be chased. People are not allowed to feed cetaceans or use sound to attract them. If people are careful when encountering cetaceans, both species can benefit.

◄ WHALE AND DOLPHIN TOURS HELP RAISE AWARENESS ABOUT THE NEED TO PROTECT CETACEANS.

Cetacean Comebacks Give Hope for the Future

During the last forty years, the humpback whale has made a fantastic comeback. Though the population has not completely recovered from commercial whaling, it has grown by the thousands. According to the International Whaling Commission, other whale populations, including blue whales and some types of right whales, are growing too.

Not all scientists accept these findings, however. It is very difficult to count cetaceans because the animals spend much of their time deep underwater and range over great distances. One thing is certain, though: cetaceans still require continued protection.

[The International Whaling Commission estimates that blue whales are increasing at a rate of about 8 percent per year.]

▶ THE HUMPBACK WHALE POPULATION IS GROWING.

You Can Help Save Whales and Dolphins

**Fun and Rewarding Ways
to Help Save Whales and Dolphins**

- Read books and articles to learn more about cetaceans.
- Visit aquariums to see cetaceans up close.
- Keep informed. Read updates on cetacean populations on the Internet. See the Internet Addresses section in the back of this book for suggestions.
- Only eat tuna and seafood with a "dolphin safe" label.
- If you live near the ocean, help out with a beach cleanup or join a whale watching group.
- Minimize your use of disposable plastics by using cloth bags and reusable containers. Plastics are a major contributor to ocean pollution.
- Write an article for your school newspaper.
- Have your class plan a fund-raiser to support cetacean conservation.

▶ YOU CAN HELP SAVE WHALES AND DOLPHINS!

GLOSSARY

Arctic—The frozen area around the North Pole.

baleen—Rows of stiff but flexible material that some whales have instead of teeth; baleen allows a whale to filter small prey from ocean water.

blowhole—An opening on a cetacean's head that it uses for breathing.

blubber—A thick layer of fat that keeps animals warm.

callosities—Thick patches of skin found on whales.

calving—The birthing process of whales.

captivity—Being in a zoo instead of the wild.

cetaceans—A group of marine mammals that includes whales, dolphins, and porpoises.

conservation—The protection of nature and animals.

cyamids—Tiny crab-like parasites, often called whale lice, that live on the skin of whales.

dorsal fin—The fin on a cetacean's back.

ecosystem—The plants and animals in an area interacting with the environment and with each other.

endangered—At risk of becoming extinct.

environment—The natural world; the area in which a person or an animal lives.

evolve—To change slowly over time.

extinct—Died out completely.

fluke—The flattened tail fin of a cetacean.

habitat—The place in which an animal lives; the features of that place including plants, landforms, and weather.

mammal—A warm-blooded animal with hair; female mammals nurse their young.

marine—Having to do with the sea.

molecule—A microscopic unit of matter made of two or more atoms.

organism—A plant or an animal.

parasite—An organism that lives on a plant or animal of another species and benefits from that host.

pollution—Substances in the air and water that harm the environment and animals that live there.

population—The total number of a group of animals.

species—A specific group of animals with shared physical characteristics and genes; members within a species can breed with each other to produce offspring.

whaling—Human hunting of whales.

Books

Gordon, David. *Uncover a Dolphin.* San Diego, CA: Silver Dolphin Books, 2008.

Gunzi, Christiane. *The Best Book of Whales and Dolphins.* New York: Kingfisher, 2006.

Kerrod, Robin. *Whales and Dolphins.* London: Lorenz Books, 2008.

Nicklin, Flip, and Linda Nicklin. *Face to Face with Dolphins.* Washington, DC: National Geographic Children's Books, 2007.

Papastavrou, Vassili. *Whale.* New York: DK Children, 2004.

Internet Addresses

Hebridean Whale and Dolphin Trust
<http://www.whaledolphintrust.co.uk>

Save the Whales
<http://www.savethewhales.org/>

Whale and Dolphin Conservation Society
<http://www.wdcs-na.org/>

INDEX